INVASION!

The
Romans

KAREN BRYANT-MOLE

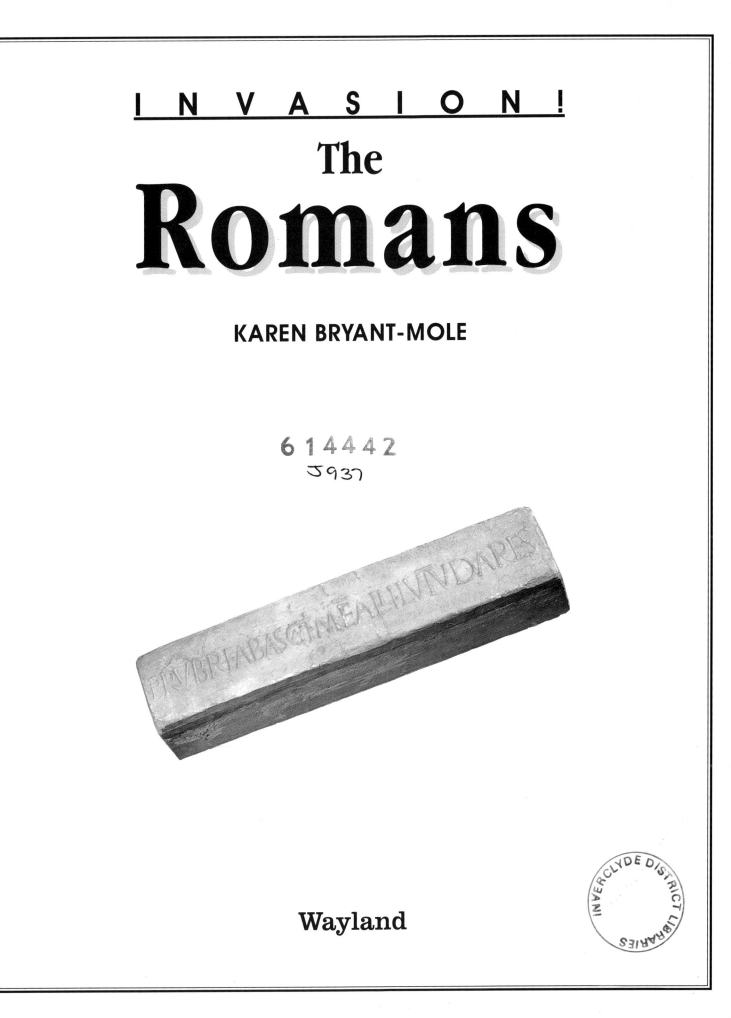

Wayland

Invasion!

The Normans
The Romans
The Saxons
The Vikings

Cover design: Simon Balley
Book design: Malcolm Walker
Editor: Deb Elliott

Text based on *Roman Invaders and Settlers* by Barry M. Marsden published by Wayland Publishers Ltd in 1992.

Picture acknowledgements
Lesley and Roy Adkins 5, 12, 13, 18 (left), 19 (left), 28; Aerofilms 23; Ancient Art & Architecture Collection cover (top left and top right); Dave Arthur 22 (top); Chester Museum 8; C.M. Dixon cover (bottom left and middle right); Michael Holford 6, 24 (left), 25 (bottom); Barry M.Marsden 11, 18 (right), 25 (top); Museum of London 20-21, 22 (bottom), 26, 27; Sheffield City Museum 24 (top); Unichrome (Bath) Ltd 19 (right); Wayland Picture Library 14; Werner Forman Archive cover (top left).
Artwork: Peter Bull 4, 9 (both), 10, 11, 14-15, 20-21, 28; Peter Dennis 7, 16-17, 23, 29 (left); Malcolm S.Walker 29 (right).

First published in 1995 by
Wayland Publishers Limited
61 Western Road, Hove,
East Sussex, BN3 1JD

British Library Cataloguing in Publication Data
  Bryant-Mole, Karen
  The Romans – (Invasion! Series)
  I. Title II. Series
  936.204

ISBN 0 7502 1469 4

Typeset by Kudos Editorial Services
Printed and bound in Italy by Rotolito Lombarda S.p.A.

Cover pictures:
Top left: A Roman relief sculpture.
Top right: A mosaic bowl.
Lower right: A clay pot showing a hunting dog.
Bottom left: A soldier's helmet and face mask.
Bottom right: A Roman coin.

Pictures opposite:
Top: Roman medical instrument.
Middle: A swimming pool at Roman baths.
Bottom: A hypocaust system.

Contents

THE CELTS 4

ROMAN SOLDIERS 6

THE ROMANS INVADE! 8

HADRIAN'S WALL 11

ART 13

TOWNS 16

VILLAS 22

ROADS, TRADE AND INDUSTRY 23

RELIGION...25

CLOTHES AND FOOD.......................26

THE ROMANS DEPART 28

GLOSSARY 30

BOOKS TO READ 30

PLACES TO VISIT 31

INDEX 32

The Celts

Before the Romans invaded Britain, the country was lived in by various tribes. These tribes are sometimes called Celts. This map shows where some of the most important Celtic tribes were based.

▲ Different groups of Celts lived in Britain before the Romans invaded.

The Celts worshipped many gods. Their priests were called druids. Celts later became Christians.

The Celts were good farmers. They used farm tools made from iron to grow a wide range of crops.

The Celts were good fighters, too. Celtic tribes often fought one another. They built hill-forts to defend their land and people. They became great warriors. But in 55BC they were to meet some even greater warriors, the Romans.

▼ These large storage jars were brought to Britain from Rome.

Roman soldiers

The Roman army was very well trained. It spread out from Rome, conquering people in its own country before invading and conquering other lands.

The Roman army was divided into legions. Each legion had about 5,500 soldiers. The soldiers were called legionaries.

A legionary wore metal armour to protect the top part of his body and a helmet to protect his head, neck and face. He carried a long spear, to throw at the enemy, and a short sword, which was used for stabbing.

Roman legionaries and the plan of a fort. ▶

◀ The Roman army had its own doctors. This is a Roman medical kit. Most of the medicines that the doctors used would have been made from herbs or other plants.

The Romans invade!

In 55BC, and again in 54BC, Julius Caesar and his army invaded the south coast of England. They defeated local tribes but did not settle in England.

Nearly a hundred years later, in AD43, about 40,000 Roman soldiers landed in southern England. They marched up to the River Thames and then on to a large settlement that we now call Colchester.

By AD47, the Romans had taken over southern England. Colchester became the capital of this Roman province.

◀ A Roman roof tile, found in England. The boar was a sign of the twentieth legion.

In the AD70s, the Romans started to advance north and west. They set up a fortress town at Chester and an army base at York. By AD84, the Romans had defeated the Scottish tribes, too. However, they did not stay in Scotland long.

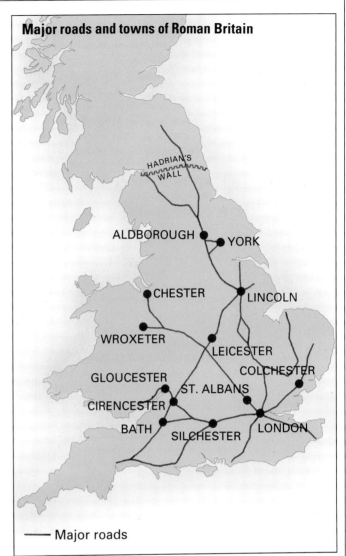

Major roads and towns of Roman Britain

—— Major roads

▲ The map above shows some of the towns and roads in Roman Britain. The longest Roman road ran all the way from Exeter to the River Humber. It is the road that passes through Bath, St Albans, Leicester and Lincoln.

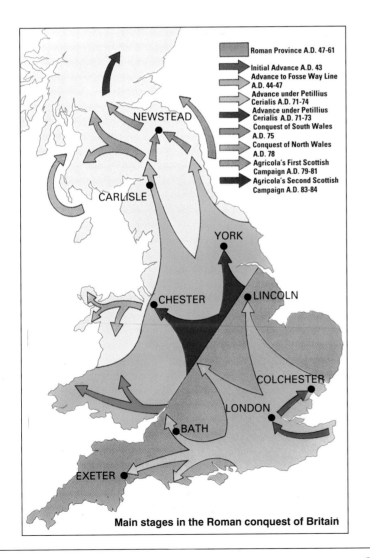

	Roman Province A.D. 47-61
	Initial Advance A.D. 43
	Advance to Fosse Way Line A.D. 44-47
	Advance under Petillius Cerialis A.D. 71-74
	Advance under Petillius Cerialis A.D. 71-73
	Conquest of South Wales A.D. 75
	Conquest of North Wales A.D. 78
	Agricola's First Scottish Campaign A.D. 79-81
	Agricola's Second Scottish Campaign A.D. 83-84

Main stages in the Roman conquest of Britain

9

Ludus Latrunculorum

This is a game that Roman soldiers played when they were off-duty. You can make it yourself. You will need modelling clay, thick cardboard, scissors, paint and a felt-tipped pen.

1 Use the clay to make twenty-four round, flat counters.
2 When the clay is dry, paint twelve of the counters.
3 Cut the cardboard into a square, 16 cm by 16 cm.
4 Divide the board into eight rows of eight squares.
5 Use the pen to colour alternate squares.

Set up the game as if you were playing draughts. Take turns to move a piece diagonally. The idea is to capture an enemy piece by trapping it between two of your own pieces.

Hadrian's Wall

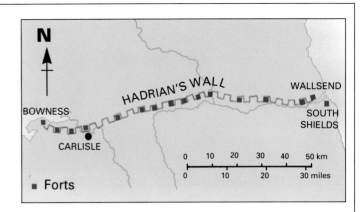

After the Romans withdrew from Scotland, the Emperor Hadrian ordered that a wall be built right across northern England.

The wall was nearly 120 km long. Every mile (about 1500 m), there was a small fort, called a milecastle. There were sixteen larger forts, too.

▲ This is a milestone on a Roman road.

▲ This picture shows you part of a fort called Housesteads. This is what it looks like today. The building you can see is the lavatory block. Roman soldiers would have washed in here.

The wall was built to mark the edge of Roman Britain and to stop Scottish tribes launching attacks. However, peaceful farmers and traders were allowed through the gates. Small towns grew up next to some of its forts.

Art

Roman artists produced sculptures, statues and paintings. The best-known Roman works of art are mosaics.

Roman mosaics were made from tiny pieces of coloured stone, tile or glass. The pieces were arranged so that they made pictures. Most mosaics were made to cover floors.

◄ This is a mosaic from Cirencester. It shows Flora, the goddess of spring.

Make part of Hadrian's Wall

You will need a baseboard and some modelling clay.

1 Cover the board with a layer of clay about 0.5 cm thick. Cut out a V-shaped ditch.

2 Make a wall about 1.5 cm high and 0.5 cm thick.

▼ This picture shows how a fort on Hadrian's Wall may have looked.

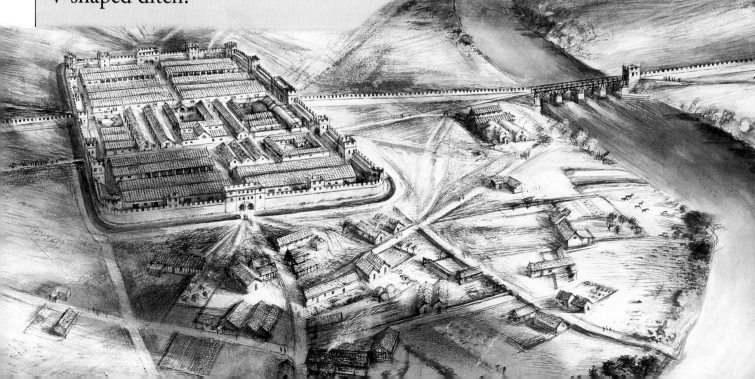

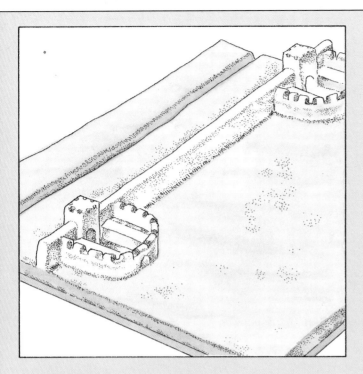

3 Build a milecastle near each end of the baseboard.

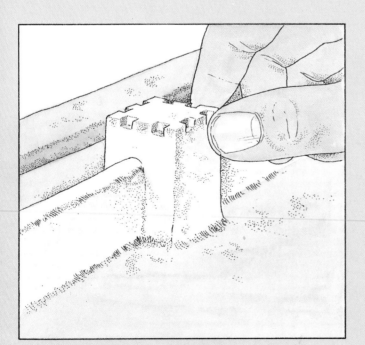

4 Place two turrets between the milecastles.

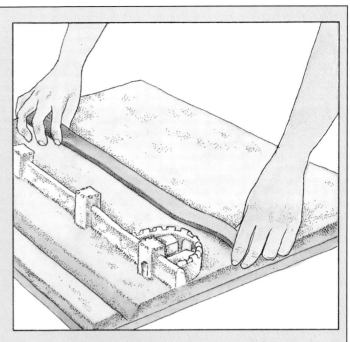

5 Lay down a 'road'.

6 Make a flat-bottomed ditch with a mound on either side. This was called a *vallum*.

Towns

This is what a Roman town might have looked like.
Roman towns were very well planned.

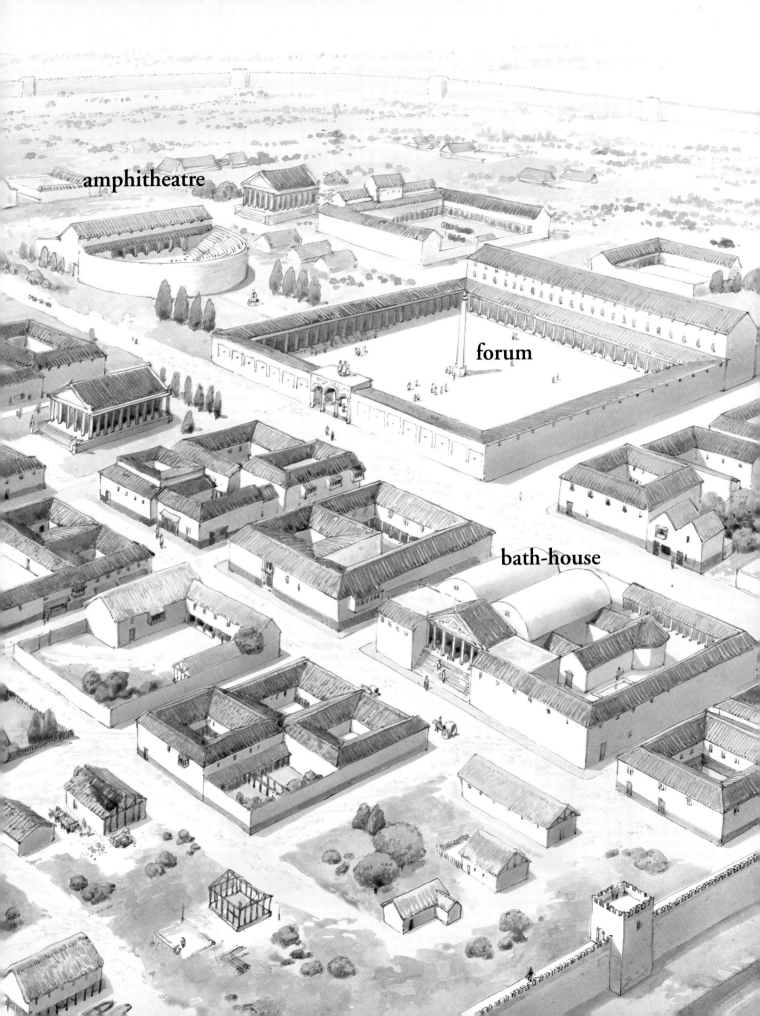

amphitheatre

forum

bath-house

In the centre of a Roman town, there was a large open space called the forum. It was a place were people could meet and pass on news. On market days, stalls were set out in the forum.

There were shops and workshops around three sides of the forum. The basilica, which was a sort of town hall, was on the fourth side.

▲ The Romans buried their dead in cemeteries along the roads going into the town. The picture above shows a Roman tombstone.

The remains of a Roman tower. ▶

Some towns had an amphitheatre. People went to the amphitheatre to watch men or animals fight.

Many towns had a bath-house, like the one above. People went through a set of pools. Each pool was a different temperature. The bath-house was a place to relax, to meet friends, to do business and even to play games.

Temples

A Roman town would have had several temples. Each temple was the house for one particular god or goddess. The altar on the left honours the god Jupiter.

Messages

The Romans wrote messages on wax tablets that could be used over and over again.

You will need some modelling clay or modelling dough.

1 Place your clay or dough on a baseboard.
2 Use a modelling tool or short knitting needle to write a message.
3 Give it to a friend to read.
4 Ask your friend to smooth out the clay or dough and write a reply.

The Romans had another way of writing messages. To try this, you will need four strips of thick card, a pen, scissors and some string.

1 Make sure that the strips of card are all the same size.
2 Make two small holes along each of the short sides.
3 Write a message.
4 Use the string to join the strips.

Your message can now be folded up, like a concertina.
Unfold it to read it.

▼ This message is scratched on a Roman tile. It is about a lazy workman called Augustalis.

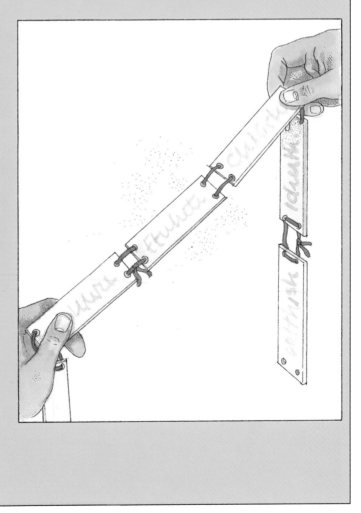

Villas

A villa was a large house in the country, usually with a farm. It had other buildings around it.

Some large villas were the homes of chieftains or rich landowners and their families. Slaves and farm workers would have had rooms in the villa, too.

The owner's private rooms were sometimes heated by hot air under the floor. These heating systems were called hypocausts. You can see what they looked like in the picture at the top of the page.

▼ This is how the dining room of a villa might have looked.

Roads, trade and industry

The Romans built a network of roads across Britain. They were built very well, like the road in the picture above. At first, they helped the invading army to move about easily. Later, they were very useful as trade routes.

A road first built by the Romans. ▶
It is still used today.

Britain became rich under Roman rule. Valuable minerals, such as gold, lead and iron ore, were mined.

This lead bar was made in ▶ Derbyshire.

Goods were traded with other countries. Britain sold grain, silver, lead and woollen cloaks. Wine, pottery, olive oil, spices and silks were brought into Britain.

◀ Ships carried goods across the Channel. These are the remains of the Roman lighthouse at Dover, that guided the ships into port.

Religion

The Romans built temples to their gods. Jupiter was one of the Romans' most important gods. He was god of the sky.

▲ The remains of a tiny temple.

Like the Celts, the Romans worshipped many different gods. They even worshipped their emperors as gods.

Most Roman families had an altar in their home, where they worshipped the gods who looked after their household.

However, as time went on, people started to become Christians. By AD400 most people in Roman Britain were Christians.

◀ The Celtic god, Sul.

Clothes and food

Ordinary people in Roman Britain usually wore tunics. These were loose, and hung to the knees. On special occasions, the Roman men who lived in Britain wore togas. A toga was a piece of cloth that was draped around the body, over the tunic.

On their feet, people wore shoes or sandals. The soles of their shoes had nailheads in them to make them more hard-wearing.

The remains of a Roman shoe and sandal. ▼

▲ A Roman kitchen may have looked like this.

Most food in Roman Britain was cooked and stored in clay pots. Kitchens had stone hearths or ovens made of clay.

Rich Romans ate very well. They sometimes held huge banquets. Country people ate local fruit, vegetables and meat. Townspeople bought their food in shops.

A Roman Banquet

Menu

First course	snails
	olives
	oysters
	peacock eggs
Main course	wild boar
	venison
	goose
	pigeon
Dessert	honey cakes
	stuffed dates
	fruit

The Romans depart

▲ Huge walls of a fort at Pevensey in Sussex.

By the end of the fourth century, the Roman Empire had become so large that it was difficult to control.

Roman legions began leaving Britain to defend other lands in Europe.

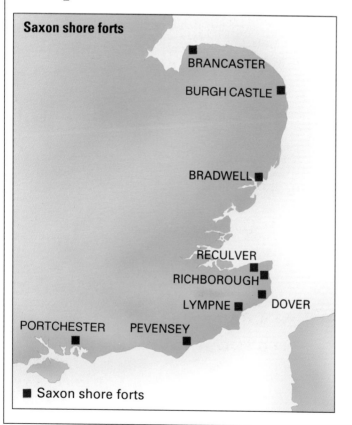

Saxon shore forts

BRANCASTER
BURGH CASTLE
BRADWELL
RECULVER
RICHBOROUGH
LYMPNE   DOVER
PORTCHESTER   PEVENSEY

■ Saxon shore forts

This left Britain open to attack. The Romans built large fortresses around the coastlines of East Anglia and southern England. They wanted to stop other people invading Britain.

Despite the fortresses, Saxons started to raid Britain. But, after the raids, they always returned to their homelands.

◄ Forts were built at these places on the coast of Britain.

28

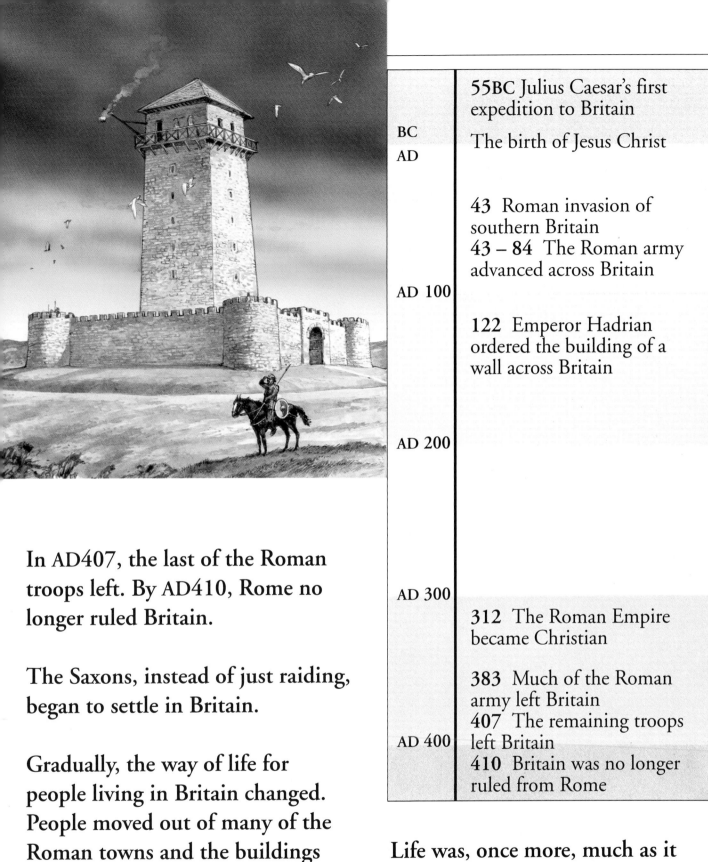

	55BC Julius Caesar's first expedition to Britain
BC AD	The birth of Jesus Christ
	43 Roman invasion of southern Britain 43 – 84 The Roman army advanced across Britain
AD 100	122 Emperor Hadrian ordered the building of a wall across Britain
AD 200	
AD 300	312 The Roman Empire became Christian
AD 400	383 Much of the Roman army left Britain 407 The remaining troops left Britain 410 Britain was no longer ruled from Rome

In AD407, the last of the Roman troops left. By AD410, Rome no longer ruled Britain.

The Saxons, instead of just raiding, began to settle in Britain.

Gradually, the way of life for people living in Britain changed. People moved out of many of the Roman towns and the buildings began to crumble. Villas, too, were deserted.

Life was, once more, much as it had been before the great Roman Invasion.

Glossary

altar   A table used when worshipping gods and goddesses.

banquet   A large meal or feast with many people.

cemetaries Places where dead people are buried.

milestones   Stones placed by the side of a road, one mile apart.

minerals   Chemicals taken from the earth by mining.

province   A part, or district, of a country.

slave   A person who is owned by another person. A slave could be bought or sold, like an animal.

tombstone   A stone used to mark the

Books to read

Everyday Life in Roman Times by Mike Corbishley (Watts Books, 1993)

Family Life in Roman Britain by Peter Chrisp (Wayland, 1994)

The Romans by Peter Hicks (Wayland, 1993)

Roman Britain by Jenny Hall and Christine Jones (BBC Educational Publishing, 1992)

Roman Britain by Gillian Osband (Kingfisher Books, National Trust, 1989)

Roman Britain by Martin O'Connell (Wayland, 1989)

Roman Cities by Roger Coote (Wayland, 1990)

Roman Soldiers by Rupert Matthews (Wayland 1989)

Places to visit

If you would like to find out more about the Romans, or see some remains of Roman Life, you could visit the following:

Aldborough in North Yorkshire: town
Baginton (The Lunt) in the West
   Midlands: reconstructed fort
Bath in Avon: public baths and site
   of a temple
Bignor in West Sussex: villa
Carnarfon in Gwynedd: fort
Canterbury in Kent: remains of a
   town house
Fishbourne in West Sussex: palace
Hadrians Wall in Northumberland
   and Cumbria
York: fortress with walls and towers

Museums
Buxton in Derbyshire
Chester in Cheshire
Cirencester in Gloucester
Colchester in Essex
Derby
Dorchester in Dorset
Hull in North Humberside
Leicester
Lincoln
London: British Museum and
Museum London
York

Index

altars 19, 25, 30
amphitheatres 17, 19
art 13

banquets 27, 30
basilica 18
bath-house 17, 19

Celts 4, 25
cemetaries 18, 30
Christians 4, 25, 29
clothes 26

doctors 6

food 27
forts 4, 9, 11–12, 14, 28
forum 18

gods and goddesses 13, 19, 25

Hadrian's Wall 11–12, 14–15, 29
hill-forts 4
hypocausts 22

legions 6, 28
Ludus Latrunculorum 10

milecastles 11, 15
milestones 11, 30
minerals 24, 30
mosaics 13

roads 9, 11, 15, 23

Saxons 28–9
shops 18, 27
soldiers 6–10, 12, 28–29

temples 19, 25
tombstones 18, 30
towns 8, 9, 12, 16–19
trading 23–4

vallum 15
villas 22, 29

warriors 4
writing 20–21